SEND!

A Dozen Ways to Make
E-mail Productive Again

PAUL H. BURTON

SEND!

A Dozen Ways to Make E-mail Productive Again

Copyright © 2013 by Paul H. Burton

Published by:
Paul H. Burton
www.quietspacing.com

Page layout by www.TheBookProducer.com

Printed in the United States of America

ISBN 978-0-9818911-9-4

DEDICATION

For those who wish to enjoy work as part
of a rewarding life.

ABOUT
PAUL H. BURTON

Paul H. Burton is a former attorney, software executive, and successful entrepreneur. He helps clients regain command of their day, get more done, and enjoy greater personal and professional satisfaction. Paul is available for keynote presentations, interactive training seminars, and individualized coaching services.

You can learn more about Paul and his work at
www.quietspacing.com.

CONTENTS

INTRODUCTION

The App We Love to Hate

E-mail. It was the killer app of the '90s. Now it's just plain killing us. We are overrun with the stuff at work. Basex, an IT and Internet research firm, reports that knowledge workers receive upward of 100 e-mails per day. Another study, conducted by Radacati, reported that business e-mail constitutes 65 percent of all e-mail sent and amounts to over one billion e-mails per day! What's worse, Radacati also reported that business e-mail usage will grow at approximately 15 percent per year into 2016. Charted, that looks like this:

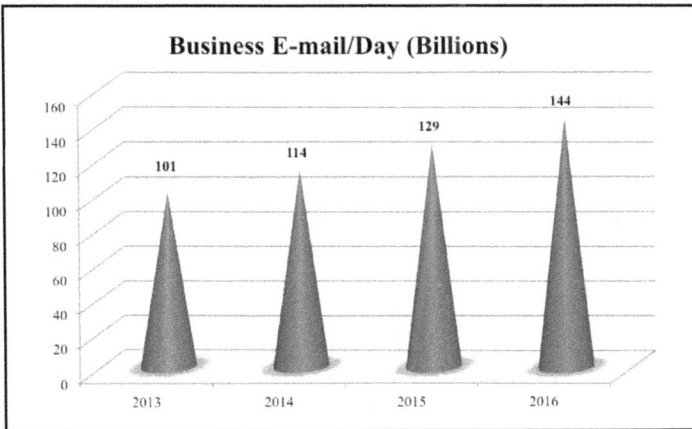

Business E-mail/Day (Billions)

Year	Value
2013	101
2014	114
2015	129
2016	144

The truth is there are very few jobs in the Internet Age that do not require the use of e-mail. It's the boon and bane of the modern world. It's the app we love to hate!

The E-mail Conundrum: Making Peace

E-mail presents us with a classic conundrum. We must use it to be productive, yet how we use it and how it affects us is often unproductive. Reducing overall volume is one piece of the puzzle, so is processing e-mails more efficiently. App developers have zeroed in on the volume issue, providing filtering services that remove or store nonessential e-mail into folders. There are also a number of software providers and training systems that address better processing for e-mail. (Shameless plug: QuietSpacing®'s "Power Processing Your E-mail" is one of the training systems.) Any combination of these options will result in better e-mail management, but that's not the point here.

The e-mail conundrum can be likened to the biblical story of Solomon's baby. King Solomon was presented with two women who claimed to be the mother of a baby. There was no objective way to determine who the baby's true mother was. King Solomon announced that the baby should be cut in half so that each woman could be satisfied. One woman announced she would forgo her claim so the baby could live. King Solomon announced that this display of compassion proved which woman was the true mother, and he awarded her the baby.

E-mail is similar. We are overwhelmed by its existence, but we must engage with it to do our work. Like King Solomon, we must find ways to use e-mail more productively so that we can enjoy our work more. That is the point here: to discover ways to make e-mail more productive and enjoyable.

Making E-mail Productive Again

What follows are 12 separate, but interrelated, suggestions for how we can make e-mail more productive again. The suggestions are broken down into two separate categories: the mechanics and the message.

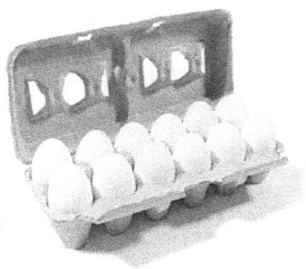

- *The Mechanics:* These six suggestions focus on when and how we use e-mail to communicate. By maximizing the *when/how* aspect of e-mail, we can be more tactical in our communications.

- *The Message:* These six suggestions focus on how to communicate *well* when using e-mail. Many e-mail users have lost the ability to communicate effectively in e-mail, which results in lost productivity and increased stressed. Small changes in the way we communicate in e-mail can alleviate many of these problems.

Each recommendation made below stands alone. You are encouraged to review them all, but only apply those you feel best suit your needs. Remember, the aggregated effects of incremental change can be surprising. For example, if we can spend thirty minutes less in e-mail each day as a result of these tips, we will spend 120 hours less in e-mail over the next year. What would you do with an additional 120 hours of available time?

OVERVIEW

Summary of Suggestions

Below is a quick overview of all twelve suggestions. Each is covered in a separate chapter to allow for quick referencing.

The Mechanics: Chapters 3-8

- *No Hiding Behind E-mail.* E-mail is good for some communications, but not all.

- *Love Reply, Loathe Reply All.* Judicious use of Reply and Reply All reduces useless e-mail traffic and the corresponding time spent managing e-mail.

- *Collective "Thank You."* Limiting unnecessary responses—"Got it," "Okay," and "Thanks"— means less e-mail for everyone.

- *Be Jekyll and Hyde.* Separating personal e-mail from work e-mail, by account, reduces temptation and distraction.

- *10-Second Rule.* Dispensing with short tasks now increases productivity, but 10 seconds is much shorter than most people think.

- *Buck Stops Here.* Sending instructions out into the ether of the Internet does not relieve the sender of responsibility.

The Message: Chapters 9-14

- *Mind the Subject Line.* The subject line is the most important part of e-mail because everyone sees it. Use it productively!

- *Give Good Signature.* A good signature line can communicate much more than just the end of the message.

- *Rules of the Road.* Abiding by certain basic rules makes the message more effective.

- *Deliver the Goods ... First.* Placing the important information at the beginning increases the likelihood of getting the results sought.

- *Be Responsalicious.* Ensuring a complete response minimizes miscommunication as well as overall (and unnecessary) e-mail traffic.

- *Write a Screenplay.* When using e-mail to delegate tasks, be clear on who's getting what.

SECTION I:

THE
MECHANICS

No Hiding Behind E-mail

E-mail is an *asynchronous* communication tool.

> **a·syn·chro·nous** *[ey-sing-kruh-nuh s]*
> adjective
> 1. *not occuring at the same time.*

Unfortunately, e-mail is regularly used as a real-time equivalent. Not convinced? Consider the number of times someone sends a second e-mail asking if the first e-mail was received. Clearly, the sender was expecting an immediate or near-immediate response.

This was never the intended use of e-mail. In fact, the best uses of e-mail are as follows:

1. To communicate information/facts.

2. To make short requests.

Whenever it's used for other types of communication (e.g., creative/developmental conversations or collaborative efforts), the threads quickly become unwieldy and unproductive. There are far better mechanisms for these types of communication.

Example: Two software developers are creating a new app called Reprise. It's a plug-in for Outlook that helps people reduce the time they spend in e-mail, making that time more productive. The developers live in different states, and each works full-time at a separate job. During the product development stages, they regularly used the following tools to make the best use of the limited time they had:

- *Skype*: Face-to-face live conversations and screen sharing.
- *Gliffy*: A cloud-based multiuser graphics tool for crafting mock-ups.
- *Dropbox*: A cloud-based file storage platform for storing and updating group files.
- *Smartphones*: For live, dynamic conversations while on the move.
- *E-mail*: For communicating updates and scheduling live conversations.

The point is that the creative and collaborative efforts were done using tools specifically designed for that purpose. E-mail was used for its best use scenario—communicating basic facts and scheduling real-time events.

(For those wondering why instant messaging isn't included above, consider this: people can speak about 150 words per minute on average, but we can only type about

50. Therefore, instant messaging is truly the worst of both worlds from a productivity standpoint. And let's not even begin to discuss the interruption issue ...)

We cannot control the actions of others, at least not as they relate to day-to-day activities. However, we have complete control over our own actions.

Exercise: To use e-mail most effectively, we need to view it as a tool for transporting factual information and making short requests. When the communication needs exceed that use, we must revert to real-time tools: the phone, video conferencing, etc. Please complete the following exercise by filling in the blanks based on what *you* are willing to do. (Note: Before answering the questions, know that recent studies have found that people do not read past the second paragraph in e-mail.)

Question	Response
How many e-mail "replies" should be allowed before a live interaction is requested?	
How many paragraphs should be allowed in an e-mail before a live interaction is requested?	

Rule of Thumb: There are no hard-and-fast rules when discussing human communication. However, combining the answers above with the following rules of thumb provides some guidance on when _not_ to use e-mail:

E-mail is _not_ the right tool in the following situations:

- The communication involves the creation or development of ideas and concepts.
- The communication is collaborative in nature.

E-mail is a fabulous asynchronous communication tool. When leveraged correctly, it's very productive.

Love Reply, Loathe Reply All

The Reply All function is used too often. There's a simple reason for this: because it's there! In other words, Reply All is used too much because we've made a habit of it. Don't buy it? Consider the following example.

Example: In Microsoft Outlook, the Reply and Reply All buttons appear next to each other in the toolbar. However, either or both of them can be moved. (In fact, they can both be eliminated completely from the toolbar, but let's not get extreme.)

Several years ago, a client moved the Reply All button to the far right side of the toolbar, quite a ways to the right of the Reply button. Within 24 hours, internal e-mail traffic went down by 20 percent!

There's only one plausible answer for this: People couldn't find it anymore, so they started hitting Reply instead. Moreover, because they were hitting Reply, they had to consider who really needed to see their reply. This reduced the volume of e-mails being sent around the office!

Still not convinced? Consider this example.

Example: Many people have Gmail accounts. In Gmail, the Reply All function is *hidden* in a drop-down menu! How could this be? Doesn't Google love us?

The answer is Google doesn't love us. They love our content. They love to mine it so they can serve us ads. That's their business model, and that's okay.

On the other hand, consider Gmail. It's a free e-mail service. It's free to you, but it costs Google lots of money. They must buy the servers, they must pay for the bandwidth, and they must hire people to manage it all. Therefore, it's in their best interest to reduce the flow of unnecessary e-mail. Reply All e-mail is often unnecessary, so Google has made finding that particular feature difficult to use by hiding it in a drop-down menu.

Rule of Thumb: Of course, Reply All has a place in e-mail. The point here is that it's not first place—it's second place. Whenever a reply is needed, stop and consider who needs to get that reply. Most times, it's just the sender and maybe one or two others. When that's the case, hit Reply and add back anyone who needs to see the reply. Occasionally, it will be everyone, in which case Reply All is appropriate.

By being mindful of which functions we're using, we can reduce the overall volume of e-mail quickly.

The Collective
"Thank You"

The old saw "The more things change, the more they stay the same" is certainly true for e-mail. The emphatic focus on response times was mentioned above, but there's another humanism that clutters up in-boxes every day: the endless "Thank you." The "Thank you" response is a cousin of the "Got it" or "Will do" response. It's an acknowledgment and expression of appreciation to the sender, neither of which are inherently bad.

Functionally, however, they're fluff. They take time to write, time to read, and time to delete. Yet nothing gets done because of them. Taken individually, they appear harmless, and the argument is that politeness has a place in e-mail. However, taken in context, they create a number of problems, especially when used in conjunction with the popular Reply All function (see the previous chapter for more on how to reduce the effects of Reply All).

Example: Let's assume that an e-mail conversation starts with just five people on the thread. As it progresses, people are hitting Reply All to communicate across the group. As the subject of the e-mail is resolved, one of the participants hits Reply All to thank everyone for their effort. This unleashes the monster! The other four people now feel compelled to respond in kind. Four additional and unnecessary e-mails are produced, which must be typed, read, and deleted by five people. That's 20 unnecessary e-mails to manage.

Rule of Thumb:* Everyone in the organization can agree up front that they appreciate the efforts of the others. By acknowledging this in real time during group gatherings, everyone can agree to stop participating in the endless "Thank you" loops.

* As a side note, this same agreement can be made with respect to the cousin e-mails mentioned above: "Got it," "Will do," "Okay," etc.

In fact, to make this more fun, why not commit to a new Unnecessary E-mail Credo? Please raise your right hand and repeat the following out loud:

Unnecessary E-mail Credo

Starting today, I will not create or participate in unnecessary e-mail threads that only serve to clutter up in-boxes around the world, so help me Internet.

Be Jekyll and Hyde

The compulsion to check our e-mail is beyond our control. Yet it's nothing new in the human experience.

Example: One hundred and fifty years ago, people would drop everything they were doing to rush into the street to meet the Pony Express rider. Fast-forward a few decades where people would dive over furniture to grab an incoming telephone call. The urgency these people felt to read a long-ago written letters or catch phone calls is no different from our modern-day urge to read an e-mail written minutes, even hours, ago.

We can't help ourselves. Or can we … ?

Rule of Thumb: Separate personal e-mail from work e-mail by creating a separate e-mail account for personal e-mail at one of the free services like Yahoo! or Gmail. Direct all personal e-mail—correspondence, personal newsletters of interest, shopping and shipping confirmations, etc.—to the new account. Check personal e-mail during down periods at work—on break, at lunch, etc.—or before and/or after work hours.

There are two benefits to this Jekyll and Hyde method: First, reducing the volume of e-mail going into the work account reduces the time spent in e-mail as well as the likelihood of unproductive distraction during the workday. In other words, we can better focus on work during work hours.

Second, during our periods away from work, especially over the weekend, two accounts means we're less likely to be drawn into work issues unless we intentionally check our work e-mail account. Consequently, we can focus on our personal lives during our personal time.

The 10-Second Rule

Thomas Jefferson once said, "Never put off for tomorrow what you can do today." David Allen, author of the popular book *Getting Things Done*, recognized how things had changed since Jefferson's time when he proposed the two-minute rule, which states, "If something takes less than two minutes, do it now."

Technology has advanced so rapidly that we must revisit Mr. Allen's two-minute rule after only a few short years. The reason is that two minutes is an eternity in e-mail. In fact, if we immediately addressed everything in e-mail that took less than two minutes, we'd never leave our inbox. The reason: today, few things in e-mail take longer than two minutes!

We need a new rule that addresses the currently reality of e-mail inundation.

Rule of Thumb: Immediately address those things in e-mail that take 10 seconds or less to accomplish. Anything that takes longer must wait until the entire batch of unread e-mail has

been read. This allows for proper priority sorting among the entire to-do list. Failure to abide by this rule results in constant firefighting because we never get a strong handle on what really needs to be done when. In other words, addressing each e-mail as it comes in leaves us in the trees, from which we never see the forest.

Implementing this rule is easy: If something in e-mail requires any level of thought, it will take longer than 10 seconds. Examples of things that take less than 10 seconds are approvals and necessary acknowledgments (see "The Collective 'Thank You,'" chapter above for more on how to handle unnecessary acknowledgments).

To get a feel for how quickly 10 seconds passes, try these three exercises:

Exercise 1:* With a stopwatch at the ready to time the exercise, get a piece of paper and a pen/pencil. (Note: A blank e-mail open and ready for completion also works.) Time yourself writing/typing the following:

Yes, I agree. Please proceed.

That will take about seven seconds, assuming there are no spelling/typing errors.

Exercise 2:* Using the same setup, time yourself writing/typing the following:

I'd like to consider this for 24 hours, okay?

That will take about ten seconds, assuming there are no spelling/typing errors.

Exercise 3:* Using the same setup, time yourself writing/typing a brief description of the most important thing you need to do today. Go!

Odds are that you had to think about what it was, then craft a concise description of it before writing/typing the answer. This simple exercise can easily take thirty seconds or more, during which other e-mails are coming in, and the immediacy of other matters continues to build.

The 10-second rule is designed to help us move through all that needs to be read and digested before we determine the now-updated priorities of the day. Getting bogged down in responding to e-mails as they come in results in lost time on other more pressing matters. In addition, clearing out the short response matters leaves only larger matters on the to-do list. In essence, the rule provides a mechanism for keeping the small things moving forward and focusing attention on the more involved projects.

---

* Remember, these exercises started with a paper/pen or an open e-mail at the ready. Precious seconds are lost each time we need to grab those instruments or hit Reply, making these results slightly skewed. In the day-to-day world, these responses take a second or two longer.

SIXTH WAY

The Buck Stops Here

Harry Truman popularized the phrase "The buck stops here." The phrase was embossed on a sign that sat atop President Truman's desk in the Oval Office. He referred to the sign and the underpinnings of the phrase on numerous occasions throughout his presidency, including his farewell address!

The fundamental message of "The buck stops here" is one of responsibility. For Truman, it was the responsibility to make decisions. For those using e-mail to pass along or delegate work, it's the responsibility to follow up.

Clicking the Send icon is a wonderful feeling. Off the item goes ... out of our world ... into the ether. Gone forever!

Or is it? Do we have any ongoing responsibility for the matters contained in the e-mail? How will we ensure any deliverables will in fact be delivered? In short, how will we follow up?

E-mail is not a closed loop system. Sending out an e-mail provides no guarantee that the recipient will do that which the e-mail requires: review the contents, perform the assignment, accept the documents, etc. If the required action is urgent, a greater risk is involved—the risk of availability. Maybe the recipient isn't near or looking at their in-box. Maybe the recipient is away from work for some period of time. The possibilities are numerous that the recipient may not see or understand what is needed in a timely manner.

Rule of Thumb: If deliverables of any kind are being transmitted by e-mail, require/ask for some form of acknowledgment from the recipient. Simply stated, get a handshake. There are a number of ways confirmation can be received, including the following:

- A confirmatory e-mail response, acknowledging/ accepting the work.
- A telephone call.
- A real-time meeting.

Note: Even after confirmation is received, ongoing responsibility for the deliverables may still rest in the sender. Consequently, some form of a tracking system must be in place to ensure the work "assigned" is completed in a timely fashion. But that's a different book (Shameless plug: see *QuietSpacing—Second Edition* at Amazon.)

SECTION II:

THE
MESSAGE

Mind the Subject Line

The Subject line is the one thing everyone sees in e-mail. Yet it is often underutilized when it comes to communicating productively using e-mail. Consider the number of e-mails that are sent with absolutely nothing in the Subject line at all! Only slightly better are the majority of e-mails that have brief and vague Subject lines. These leave recipients to guess at the contents until the e-mails are actually opened and read.

Examples: Here are some recent examples of e-mails actually received:

Subject:	

Subject:	long time since we talked

Come now. We can do better, can't we? Of course we can!

A look back into the past provides some guidance. Specifically, the structure of a business letter delivers an answer. Back when business letters were used to communicate information, they took several standard forms. In them appeared the Date and the Addressee block. Right below that came the RE: line. The RE: provided a brief description of the contents appearing below.

SHAZAM!

Isn't the Subject line in e-mail the same thing as the RE: line in ole-timey letters? Yes, egad, it is! What if we adopted the same conventions used for the RE: line?

Rule of Thumb: Make the most of every Subject line in e-mails sent. Use brief descriptive language to communicate the contents of the e-mail's body. Reference the project, include related action items and deadlines, and use spaces, symbols, and characters (e.g., = + ; , −) to help the reader quickly review and understand what the e-mail is about. Adopt a series of shorthand references like EOM (end of message) or NRN (no response necessary) for use when it's appropriate.

Don't these look better?

Subject:	Did you bill credit cards? EOM

Subject:	coordinating Bite-Sized Booklet · Deliverables & Deadline = PHB creates first draft by 4/30

For extra credit, consider adopting these e-mail subject matter principles:

For extra credit, consider adopting these e-mail subject matter principles:

- *Subject Line Updates:* Whenever the conversation within the e-mail changes, change the Subject line to reflect the new subject. Better yet, just start a new e-mail! Either way, keeping an old Subject line in place when a new thread develops is likely to create confusion.

- *Super-FYI'ing:* Whenever an e-mail is forwarded to a new recipient with the intention of FYI'ing the new recipient, either (a) append the Subject line with why the FYI is being sent or (b) provide an introductory sentence in the body of the forwarded e-mail directing the new recipient's attention to the point being made.

The Subject line is a perfect place to communicate a tremendous amount of information to the recipient in an effective and productive manner. Everyone sees the Subject line, so let's make good use of it.

Give Good Signature

How often do we dig around in the in-box hoping to find a particular person's contact information at the bottom of one of their e-mails? All the time. The in-box has become the repository for all things work related for many people. Part storage vault, part to-do list, part contact database, and part communication tool—the in-box serves many functions.

So why are so many e-mails devoid of this key information? Not only can it be automatically included in every e-mail, it's also highly valuable information that senders should ensure gets communicated often! Not only does including a good signature block assist those looking for our contact information, it also provides a platform to communicate all kinds of information.

Example: Sometimes the gods shine down on us all. The following signature block appeared in the author's inbox while writing this book. With the sender's permission, here is a perfect example of how to give good signature.

Contact Info	Roxann Lincoln AP / AR Manager Cavaliers Operating Company, LLC. 1 Center Court Cleveland, Ohio 44115 Tel: (216) 420-2041 Fax: (216) 420-2223 Email: RLincoln@cavs.com http://www.cavs.com http://www.lakeeriemonsters.com http://www.clevelandgladiators.com http://www.theqarena.com http://www.cantoncharge.com
Promotional Info	 Sat. May 11 - Gladiators vs. Chicago Rush Sat. May 18 - Gladiators vs. San Antonio Talons Sun. June 9 - New Kids On The Block - 98 Degrees - Boyz II Men Fri. June 14 - Cleveland Crush vs. Omaha Heart Sat. June 15 - Fleetwood Mac Live 2013
Social Connect	Become a Q INSIDER and get special presale offers for events at The Q. Click here to sign up.
Additional Info	QUICKEN LOANS ARENA EVENTS Phone: 1-888-894-9424 In Person: Quicken Loans Arena and All Northern Ohio Discount Drug Marts. Online: www.theQarena.com

This signature block is right for all the reasons highlighted. Anything a recipient might need is contained in this auto-populating feature.

Rule of Thumb: Use the signature block in each e-mail sent to communicate vital contact and other important information to facilitate the recipient's receipt and use of that information in the future. Further, use the auto-include feature contained in most e-mail software to make the inclusion of this information simple. As a guideline, consider including the following information:

- Name, e-mail address, phone number, firm name, website address.
- Recent good stuff: awards, publications, other marketing and branding information.
- Offers, if any.
- Social networking connections.

As a word of caution, consider closely whether any political, environmental, or other stance is well suited for business communications. Many people include these items in their e-mail signature block. Though well intended, they can also easily backfire. Just a word of caution.

Rules of the Road

Quality is often a casualty of the instant-response culture that surrounds e-mail. Immediacy can be good, but not when accuracy suffers. Moreover, quality goes deeper than mere substantive accuracy. Both form and professionalism matter too. All too often, these additional spokes on the wheel of quality are cast aside in the name of speed.

If accuracy is the price of admission—meaning competitors can provide the same information—then form and professionalism can set an e-mail sender apart from the rest. Many take the position that the correct answer and the speed of response are the ultimate determinants. That's true for game shows, but this isn't a game show. In the business world, delivering the correct answer in a well-formed and professional manner will always rule the day over right but sloppy.

Example: A client tells an embarrassing story to make this point. He had been e-mailing with a business associate about an upcoming event. The thread turned a bit cavalier given the strong relationship between

the two of them. Unfortunately, at a later point, a third party—the decision maker—was looped into the thread. Explaining what was actually meant during the earlier course of the communication was a bit embarrassing for everyone. In hindsight, remembering that business communications dictate a different level of attention was the better choice.

Rules of Thumb: There are several formatting and professional factors to consider before hitting Send for any e-mail.

- *Always Be Professional.* Maintaining a professional tone is vital to delivering a professional product. Being formal may not be necessary. In fact, being authentic is always preferred, but familiarity should be reserved for personal correspondence and only with the closest of business colleagues.

- *Grammar and Spelling.* No matter how urgent the response is needed, good grammar and correct spelling are mandatory. Communications failing this standard demonstrate a fundamental lack of ability. The substantive accuracy comes into question when a sender can't get these communication fundamentals right.

- *Pace, Clarity, and Completeness.* These three items go to the readability of the communication. Pace speaks to the rate at which the recipient can digest the information. Clarity focuses on delivering the substantive answer in a concise and cogent manner. Completeness is about addressing all the points associated with the communication, leaving nothing unanswered.

- *No Yelling.* In e-mail, the use of ALL CAPS suggests the sender is yelling. There is never a place for this in business e-mail.

- *Brevity Is Beautiful.* There are lots of good writing tips and tricks. Here are a couple of particular merit:

  - Keep sentences shorter than 25 words to keep the reader focused.

  - Eliminate intensifiers ("really," "very," "clearly," etc.) as little value is added, but length suffers.

  - Always consider swapping the word after an "of" with the word before an "of" to see if the "of" can be eliminated.

- *Read, Pause, Send.* Before hitting Send, always read what's been written and pause to consider it from a holistic perspective (is everything covered correctly *and* professionally?).

Following a few simple rules for how to craft and communicate in e-mail will increase the effectiveness of these communications.

TENTH WAY

Deliver the Goods ... First

We have less time than we used to. That's a simple reality of the modern 24x7 business world. One result is people don't have as much time to read everything thoroughly. In fact, recent studies indicate people ***don't read past the second paragraph in e-mail***!

Not only do we need to communicate professionally, we also need to find ways to communicate effectively (and productively) under these conditions. The bottom line is that we have to move away from the typical narrative style of writing e-mails and move to an outline or memo style.

Example: The author was once the general counsel for a software company. As such, he regularly interacted with the CEO. All roads led to Maureen, the CEO's administrative assistant, for face time with the CEO. On more than one occasion, Maureen would interrupt the author's explanation of the reasoning for a meeting with "Conclude, Paul. Conclude." This was usually delivered with a smile, but the point was made all the same.

Rule of Thumb: Adopt an outline or memo style of writing to ensure recipients are (a) seeing and (b) getting what they need from your e-mail.

- Put conclusions, observations, and requests for action first.
- Use lists and bullet points.
- Craft short, crisp sentences and paragraphs to encourage reading.
- Supporting information goes at the bottom.

Here are some examples of these suggestions:

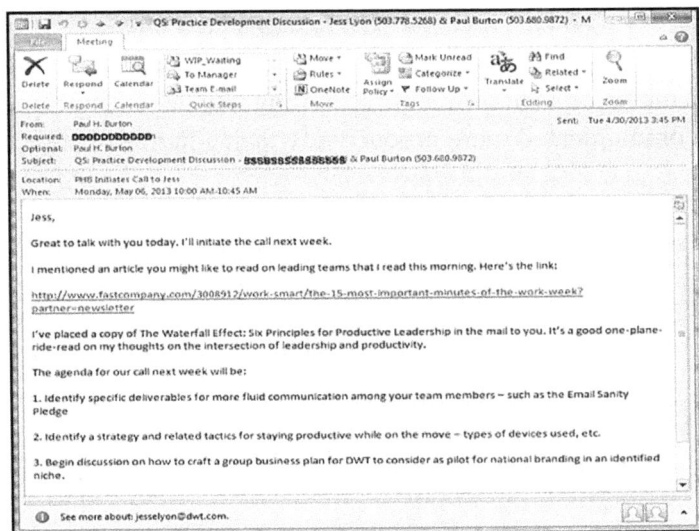

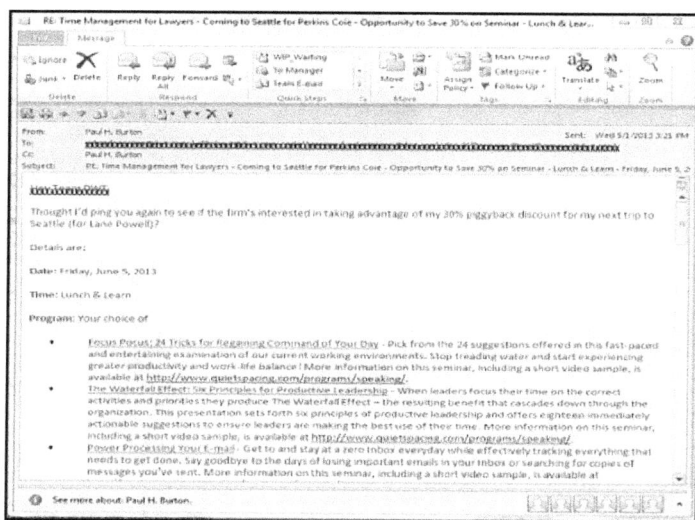

The point of sending an e-mail is to communicate. Using a memo or an outline style of writing will get the message communicated more productively than a narrative style.

ELEVENTH WAY

Be Responsalicious

Responding to e-mail is an art form in itself. Most people treat it as though a real-time conversation is taking place, which would allow for a dynamic exchange of information. The problem is that a reply to a message may come minutes, hours, or even days after the original e-mail was sent. Complicating matters further, there's no guarantee that the original sender will see the reply anytime soon. The list of pitfalls under these circumstances include the following:

- Misunderstanding the original message.
- Failing to completely respond to the original message.
- Misunderstanding the response of the original sender due to the passage of time or inartful phrasing.

When this happens, senders and repliers generally devolve into an unproductive e-mail exchange that seeks to clarify the situation. Stress levels go up, and time is wasted.

Rule of Thumb: Treat e-mail more like letter writing than conversation. Most people refer back to the original correspondence regularly when replying to a letter. This serves the purpose of ensuring that the response aligns with the original message. Include this checklist of items when replying to e-mail to be responsalicious:

- Answer *all* questions asked.
- Categorize/separate subjects addressed or answered (see "Deliver the Goods ... First" above for examples).
- Append the Subject line with a descriptor of your reply. Examples include "Revised" or "Update" at the beginning of the Subject line or add some language to the end of the Subject line that briefly summarizes your input.
- Never add a new subject matter to an existing thread. Start a new e-mail to avoid confusion.
- Pick up the phone or schedule a meeting if clarification is needed.

One of the greatest ways to make e-mail more productive is by writing complete and clear responses. Real-time conversation may be necessary to clarify the original message, but they are a waste of time if used to clear up misunderstandings resulting from poor replies.

TWELFTH WAY

Write a Screenplay

Communicating via e-mail to a group of people is fraught with risk. Information must be passed along to everyone, but many times, only a few people need to take action. Getting mired in an unnecessary thread of replies attempting to clarify the original intent can be avoided if the e-mail is crafted like a screenplay.

Screenplays follow a strict format. Description and background information are set out in narrative form. Dialogue is indicated typographically and visually. Here's an example:

The dark forest is lit only by a pale moon. Dick and Jane are searching for the shelter of an abandoned cabin located somewhere nearby. They have become separated from each other.

DICK
Jane? Jane, can you still hear me?

JANE
Yes! Your voice is coming from my right.

Both information and background are clearly set apart from the dialogue. In addition, each actor knows which lines of dialogue are his or hers. No confusion. Simple.

Rules of Thumb: Applying a screenplay format to group e-mails is also simple.

- *Information for All.* Open the e-mail with information everyone needs to know.
- *Use Directives to Identify Action or Important Information.* Start a new paragraph to separate action items or other important information. Then lead with a person's name or descriptor of the information.

Example: This is what a well-written e-mail to a group can look like:

We are scheduled to close on the Johnson transaction next week. I want to remind everyone how important this is for us, and I want to thank you all in advance for helping us to make this a successful event.

Questions: If anyone has any additional questions, please direct them to me in a separate e-mail.

Closing Information: The closing is scheduled for Conference Room A at 2:00 p.m. next

Thursday. Those required to attend are Dick, Jane, and myself.

Dick: Please send me drafts of the documents no later than this Friday at 12:00 p.m. Please reply only to Jane and me with the drafts.

Jane: Please confirm with the Johnson team that they know where the closing is taking place. Also, let them know we'll have the final documents to them by Tuesday for their review. Please reply only to me when this is done.

By employing this format, the information is communicated to everyone, and those with specific action items know who they are. Moreover, by clarifying how to reply and how to make inquiries, unnecessary e-mail traffic is eliminated.

E-mail Is Forever

There is one final message to convey before closing this narrative. Unlike conversations that occur in real time and are subject to the vagaries of memory, e-mail is much more like letters in one important way:

E-mail Is Forever

Rule of Thumb: Before hitting the Send button, stop and ask yourself if what is contained in the e-mail (original or reply) you have just written will stand the harsh light of scrutiny sometime in the future. Electronic discovery tools have become expert at ferreting out many smoking guns lying dormant in e-mail communications.

Those who don't follow this rule of thumb hit Send at their own peril.

CONCLUSION

It's Here to Stay

E-mail isn't going anywhere soon. We will likely be dealing with this tool we love to hate for the rest of our careers.

Using the best practices discussed above will result in better use of e-mail. Communication will be clearer, there will be lower volume, and stress levels will be reduced. However, if you don't want to deal with it at all, there are still some opportunities in fields that don't rely on e-mail...

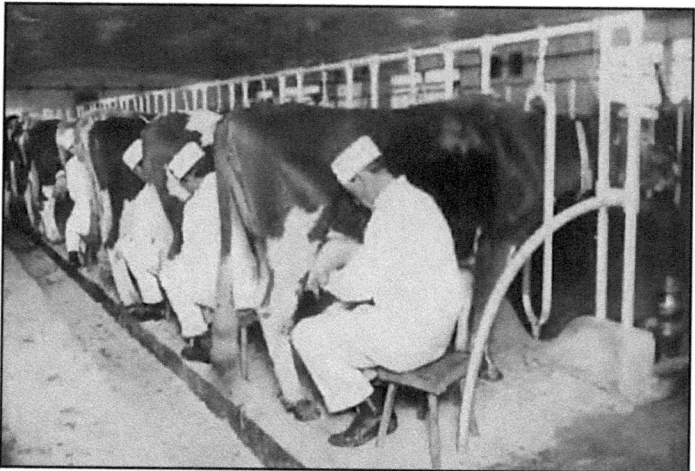

www.ingramcontent.com/pod-product-compliance
Lightning Source LLC
Chambersburg PA
CBHW071335200326
41520CB00013B/2992